BEFORE YOU BEGIN...

Make sure to download the FREE audio program for this book which comes with your purchase! Just go to

www.slangman.com/audio

then look for your book and enter this code:

E2C2YW8NIZ3T

GOLDILOCKS and the 3 BEARS

Written by: David Burke
Copy Editor: Julie Bobrick
Illustrated by: "Migs!" Sandoval
Translators: Li Li Peters & Ming Tao
Proofreaders: Lin Zhu & Connie Sun

Copyright © 2017 by David Burke

Email: info@heywordy.com
Website: www.heywordy.com

Hey Wordy! and all related characters and elements are © and trademarks of Hey Wordy, LLC.

ISBN13: 978-1-891888-24-3

Printed in the U.S.A.

Meet the Author
David Burke

Creator and star of the children's TV show, *Hey Wordy!*, David Burke has been single-handedly revolutionizing the foreign language-learning movement worldwide.

In addition to being a performer of boundless energy and enthusiasm, David speaks seven languages. A successful author and entrepreneur, he has built a thriving international publishing company featuring over 100 books he has written for teen/adults & children. His books have won publishing awards and have sold more than one million copies. David's Street Speak™ and Biz Speak™ series of books and audio programs are used around the world by government agencies, leading universities and major corporations.

Since age 4, David has been a classically trained pianist and uses his musical gifts to compose and perform original songs for his TV series, *Hey Wordy!* which introduces children to foreign languages and cultures through music, animation, and magical adventures. He has also composed, orchestrated, and performed all the music in the audio programs for each of these books.

David's engaging and charismatic persona became a fixture on broadcast entertainment channels around the world, such as CNN and the BBC. David and his work have been highlighted in many major publications, including The Los Angeles Times, The Chicago Tribune and The Christian Science Monitor.

"This series teaches everyday words that occur in your child's life, as well as terms having to do with politeness, greetings, family & friendship."

David Burke

Chinese vocabulary taught:

baobao = *baby*
chuang = *bed*
chufang = *kitchen*
er = *two*
leile = *tired*
leng = *cold*
men = *door*
re = *hot*
ruan = *soft*
san = *three*

sanbu = *walk*
wan = *bowl*
xiao = *little*
xiong = *bear*
xiong baba = *papa bear*
xiong mama = *mama bear*
yi = *one*
yizi = *chair*
ying = *hard*
zhuozi = *table*

A few things to remember...

- In this fairy tale, you'll notice that some of the words in Chinese are reversed! This is very normal in many languages. For example:

  papa bear = **xiong baba** (literally, "bear papa")
  mama bear = **xiong mama** (literally, "bear mama")
  baby bear = **xiong baobao** (literally, "bear baby")

- The words in *green italics* throughout this fairy tale are words you've already learned in the previous level! Do you still remember what they mean?

from Cindellera (Level 1)

buyong keqi = you're welcome
da = big
fangzi = house
gaoxing = happy
huai = mean
jiao = foot
nuhaizi = girl
piaoliang = pretty
qizi = wife

qunzi = dress
shangxin = sad
wangzi = prince
wuye = midnight
wuhui = party
xiezi = shoe
xiexie ni = thank you
yingjun = handsome
zaijian = goodbye

1

xiong ←
(熊)
xiong baba ←
(熊爸爸)
xiong mama ←
(熊媽媽)

Once upon a time, there was a (bear) family. The **xiong** family lived in a *fangzi* in the forest – a (papa bear) who was the head of the household, a (mama bear) who was very *piaoliang*,

and a little **xiong** who was their baby.
The **xiao xiong baobao** was very *yingjun*
like his **baba**. Needless to say, the **xiong**
baba and the **xiong mama** were very

xiao
(小)
baobao
(寶寶)

3

proud of their **xiong** family. One day, the **xiong mama** prepared some soup for lunch, but it was too hot. While it cooled off, the **xiong** family went for a stroll.

sanbu
(散步)

Meanwhile in a town nearby, there lived a **nuhaizi** named Goldilocks who was very **shangxin** because she was so tired of never having anything fun to do.

5

She thought for a moment and decided to take a **sanbu** in the forest. Very soon, she came upon a *fangzi* and knocked on the [door] but no one

men
(門)

was there. So she opened the **men**, put one *jiao* inside the *fangzi*, and said "Hello? Is anyone home?" She was very tired after her long **sanbu**

leile
(累了)

7

and since no one answered, she walked inside the *fangzi*. She looked around and was very *gaoxing* to see a table in the kitchen with food on it!

zhuozi
(桌子)
chufang
(廚房)

8

She quickly approached the **zhuozi** in the **chufang** and was super extra *gaoxing* because there on the **zhuozi** in the **chufang** was a [bowl] —

wan
(碗)

9

yi (一)

er (二)

san (三)

but not just one **wan**. There were one, two three of them! **Yi**, **er**, **san** sitting on the **zhuozi**. And something smelled so good! She took a taste from the **wan** that belonged

to the **xiong baba** and said, "This is too hot!" ➤ **re**
(熱)

Then she took a taste from the **wan** that

belonged to the **xiong mama** and said,

"This is too cold!" Then she took a taste from ➤ **leng**
(冷)

the **xiao wan** of the **xiao xiong baobao** and
said, "Ah. This one isn't too **re**. It isn't too **leng**.
It's just right!" And she ate everything in the
xiao wan. "*Xiexie ni!*" she said to the empty

wan. Well, now she was even more **leile**
than ever after eating so much food.
So, she decided to rest. In the living
room, she saw a [chair]...but not just

yizi
(椅子)

13

one **yizi**. There were **yi**, **er**, **san** of them! **Yi**, **er**, **san**! So, she sat down in the **yizi** of the **xiong baba** and said, "Oh! This **yizi** is too [hard]!"

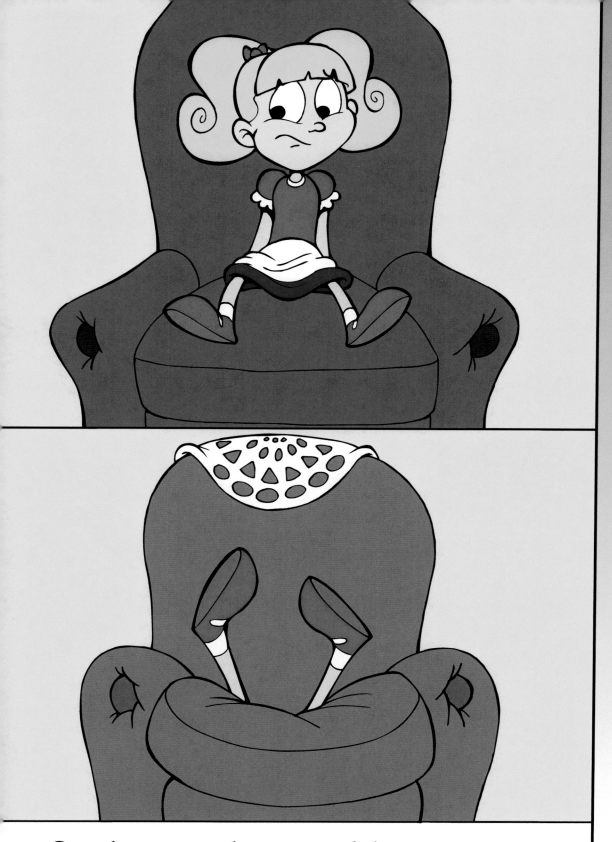

So, she sat in the **yizi** of the **xiong mama** and said, "Oh! This **yizi** is too [soft]!" Then she sat in the **xiao yizi** of the **xiao xiong baobao** and said,

ruan
(軟)

15

"Ahhhhh. This **yizi** isn't too **ying**. It isn't too **ruan**. It's just right!" But just as she got comfortable, *CRACK!* The **xiao yizi** broke and completely fell apart!

Still **leile**, she decided to look for the bedroom to take a **xiao** nap. In front of her, she saw a [bed]... but not just one **chuang**. There were **yi**, **er**, **san** of them!

chuang
(床)

Yi, **er**, **san**! So, she tried the **chuang** of the **xiong baba**, but it was too **ying**. Then she tried the **chuang** of the **xiong mama**, but it was too **ruan**. Finally, she tried the

18

xiao chuang of the **xiao xiong baobao** and said, "Ahhh. This **chuang** isn't too **ying**. It isn't too **ruan**. It's just right!" And she fell asleep. At that moment,

the **xiong** family returned from their **sanbu**. As soon as they walked in, the **xiong baba** noticed something strange. "Someone's been eating my soup!"

said the **xiong baba**. "And someone's been
eating my soup!" said the **xiong mama**.
"And someone's been eating MY soup and
ate it all up!" cried the **xiao xiong baobao**.

"Look!" said the **xiong baba**. "Someone's been sitting in my **yizi**!" Then the **xiong mama** said, "And someone's been sitting in my **yizi**, as well!"

"And someone's been sitting in my **xiao yizi** and broke it into pieces!" cried the **xiao xiong baobao**. Suddenly, the **xiong baba**, the **xiong mama**, and the

xiao xiong baobao heard snoring coming from the bedroom, so they went in to look. "Someone's been sleeping in my **chuang**!" said the **xiong baba**. "And

someone's been sleeping in my **chuang** as well," said the **xiong mama**. "And someone's been sleeping in my **xiao chuang** and there she is!" shouted the

25

xiao xiong baobao. Just then, Goldilocks woke up and was surprised to see the **xiong** family! The **xiong** family thought the **xiao nuhaizi** was very *huai* to use their *fangzi*

without permission! So, Goldilocks said
to the **xiong baba**, "Oh, *xiexie ni* for
letting me eat food from your **wan**, sit
in your **yizi**, and lie in your **chuang**!

Xiexie ni!" She expected the **xiong** family to say, "*Buyong keqi!*" But they were angry that she caused so much trouble in their *fangzi* and the **xiong** family growled

at her. So, she slowly stood up on the **chuang** of the **xiao xiong baobao**, and nervously said, "Well, *xiexie ni* for everything and... *Zaijian*!" And with that, Goldilocks

jumped off the **xiao chuang**, and dashed out the front **men**, running as fast as each *jiao* could move. Needless to say, she never returned to visit the *fangzi* of the **xiong** family again.

Made in the USA
Middletown, DE
21 December 2021

56794424R00022